Praise for
Cartoon Logic, ~~Cartoon Violence~~

Every single poem in Alexus Erin's *Ca~~rtoon Logic, Cartoon Violence~~* comes directly from the mouth. This is an important voice that makes us question what happens when we hold on tighter to the ever-passing commercials and pixelated cartoons, questioning and voicing our true realities, especially in the contexts of violence and injustice. Erin's full-length debut is an ars poetica that makes us jump into love—this is a book of constant focal points and priceless camera asides—it will make you hungry.

— **Dorothy Chan,** *Revenge of the Asian Woman*

In *Cartoon Logic, Cartoon Violence*, Alexus Erin transmogrifies her sure-tongued words into Acme-type explosives, defying physics to puncture reality's patchwork. From the star-shaped holes her poems cut, golden hour light illuminates divinity in stillness and brutality: holy incense rising from a post-prom coffee, the hollow erasure that comes with grief, and the gut-punch pleasures of choral chord changes and pop-punk push pits. Her sleight-of-hand etymological slicing makes detours for Medieval cantatas, 1960s sit-coms, dreams, dances, desserts, and so much more—a giddy trajectory that traces lucid, crucial messages in smoke across the bright celluloid sky.

— **Sadie Dupuis of Speedy Ortiz and Sad13**

In *Cartoon Logic, Cartoon Violence*, Alexus Erin shows the heartbeat beyond the pixels of human perception to the pains and joys therein. These poems journey, with a relentlessly curious and personal speaker's voice, from loss to body image to the multifaceted Black experience. In this book, we are illuminated as if on a technicolor screen. We vibrate with inescapable life.

— **Ashley M. Jones,** *REPARATIONS NOW!*

Alexus Erin's words defy gravity. Not just in their elastic critique of how the world runs out of road for Black folks, but in the stretching of space & logic. In this brilliant debut collection, *Cartoon Logic, Cartoon Violence*, Erin's poems push past the limitations of this dimension & offer a close-eyed intimate navigation of a world by hand. We watch the hands drawing the boundaries of this world with Erin's words, it's positioning, it's havoc . . . This collection is electric.

— **Nabila Lovelace,** *Sons of Achilles*

Cartoon Logic, Cartoon Violence

Cartoon Logic, Cartoon Violence

poems

Alexus Erin

BAOBAB PRESS

First Printing

ISBN-13: 978-1-936097-39-5
ISBN-10: 1-936097-39-7

Library of Congress Control Number: 2021939043

Baobab Press
121 California Ave
Reno, Nevada 89509
www.baobabpress.com

Cover Art/Photo © 2022 Kimberly Gordon

In loving memory of

my father, Stephen Davis
&
my stepfather, Franklin Woods

Logic

Violence

Any body suspended

2. Any _____ in motion

inter-
venes

passing
through solid matter

time required

equal to

capture _____ unbroken.

gravity

negated by fear.

Certain bodies _____ pass
through solid walls

others cannot.

violent rearrange-
ment _____ im-
permanent.

we need the relief

instead.

Logic

A Partial List, in Case of Emergency

I cannot tally the reasons
to rejoice.
They, then, count themselves
independent insomuch as
there is still
a child I used to care for, asking about the manger babe, downtown,
mid-spring, his fever fading
in and out.
Here, near Broughty Ferry, and speeding further south—
rurals of a different country:
A tracing touch in the Doolin pub, before any threat of scorn
Heat caught in sprung floors—marley at the studio,
where we turn and roll
Holly branch, waxen and out of its season
Leo leaping the back of a UPS truck, throwing
his scooter in the pond, unable to keep a straight face
at the front door,
asking my mother if I could come out to play.
My dancers are still at the foot of the bed, in a straight line,
waking me for Fosse. Time living through them,
in any blurred longueur: the sepia afternoons I am nearly deaf to my name
as it is called by friends who want to know
where I went the moment I stopped speaking
Interrupted
by a kookaburra
I saw in 2004
A punk show Junes ago, returning
Home, in one way I have understood it—giving thanks.
It has been my dream to work and love this way
To honor snare ruckus in all weather, my fuzzy microphone
Moments that held me in momentary sway, thrown
by awe or rapture
Knocked damn-near-all-the-way-out
Until I was not entirely flightless, but shortened
to the space of a credible presence.
Being,
and taking in quick
spurts of air

On a Monday, June 9th, 2015

Sometimes, when I think about love,
I do the math.
Calculate dispersion:
the word, from
feeling, from the
work. On a bus from the Bronx,
back to where Brooklyn starts,
in a borrowed dress
and purse, with no thought-out plan
as to where I should spend the night
Measuring distance from design, big designer,
I watched the sky as though this had been the plan
all along —
it could have been
to isolate them in the stretched shade
obstructing Holzer's Truisms,
projected on the reception hall
behind a garden of dahlias
In a crowd of mostly women,
dressed like Frida Kahlo to celebrate
Which gave me hope, of course.
Above
the koi pond
at midnight
stood a silhouette shadow,
an embrace.
20 ft away from a humming projector:
the single source of all the light we had.
I watched this in good threes, too:
the pair, visible by a rogue fluorescent ray
First blurred body, then upside down in the meniscus of my drink
Retrospection in a near future:
through coach window,
revelatory, a newfound distance —
how many degrees
of freedom
do you sleep
from the truth,

another?
Variable of one, doubled
in the water bath that housed
all the pretty fish,
reflected,
rippling

This Must Be the Place (Or, Walking Home, I am Reminded to Buy Champagne and Overalls)

I.
I was cooking to make house home
and wearing dark green, floating Grafton Street
phantasmic, buying flowers to top all the Thanksgiving dishes.
It stalked,
dressed in suede and maroon—I hardly ever thought to run.
In fact, I forgot captivity for weeks on end
(This makes sense—busy is busy,
and we're busy people: when Maya Angelou passed,
we just pretended she *hadn't*
Willed the harried solemn to be evidence of standard protocol—
the room held no new weight. No time
to mourn
To consider our own liberation, as she would have wanted.
Smoothing spread on the crackers, we ignored the fissures
their rough-ground salt grains made on the spackled layer)
The nightmare
before the nightmare:
it made habit of asking, night after night, if I was afraid
Pressing boundaries, granted their existence, on anything venial. Its breathing,
mixed with the sound of the radiator
Talk,
radiator.
It attended the oven, sprinkling petals in all the food, as I had requested,
sneery and splitting the baked macaroni
between with peas and without; dragging a jagged line through the mush
in the glass dish, borrowed from who-knows-where
with a spoon I had never seen before
But with it,
I soon became familiar

II.
I cannot guarantee
these are comparable in natural light.
It, still, isn't easy for me: I watched myself

clean the bad jokes off the stove after dinner. Which is to say,
I cleaned extortion from the stove
after dinner
Often out-of-body
The stove, itself, maybe thinking
"they endured"
Like family can
To save itself, I mean
To outdo the familiar
To build a reference point
Better, sometimes,
there were days I lived with strangers. We only knew three chords
To riff apart the quiet
Medley every song we knew could fit
A lengthening afternoon, waiting to sing, free:
"When you walk in the room, I see things that I can't understand
I want you endlessly"

III.
A word on home:
There is my mother, definitely overdoing it with the sugar cane
Bunched and bought, crowding the counter
of a childhood, one and only
Roots, shoots, a bag of ginger
Joint junctures thready, akimbo
Home, a codeword for
our school bus stopped in the rain
Beckoning the geese, we are lit up inside from the floodlight. This new
ontological positioning:
late for school, thus defying natural order, traffic, time
or, 1999—
crawling, confident, toward Naomi Shihab Nye,
who sat in a chair in the middle of the sea-coloured carpet, reading poems aloud
in the Lower School music room
where I loved to listen to songs about God: testimony echolocating
an early signal to persevere
In Christ: a new creation. Which is to say, with grace
wash, rinse, repeat
Good method into ritual

Ritual to method, learned more
cure, or,
It is certainly enough
for today: willing only one thing
To transcend the comforts of the state—this must be the place
To sleep, to work, to celebrate

Reading Up on Diane Arbus

After Rob's family photo

You were smaller then, smaller than I actually
knew you could be.
You are fields, favorite songs.
You, precious filament.
You didn't know how to camera smile. Or maybe the sun was in
your eyes. Or God was moving through you
at paces only those bound in such flight can calculate.

Rolled down to your ankles are a pair of green socks that match
your sister's winter coat.
Your father is laughing soundless from his stomach.
Mother is as pillars are: graced, ageless, reflecting the sun
You were everything you ever touched: the snow, patched and full of
February, paint chips from the Presbyterian Church;
its dark windows, a second story with tiny
palm-printed smudges. I imagine, now, all the bodies
packed horizontal in the upper room, and shake.
Please. We're so blessed. I don't want to be afraid
I don't want to believe that we are all at the mercy of one another's deaths.

We wrinkle the hem of Second Chance
with shrinking fingers and I know we're only getting younger.
In our mouths, stretched sideways by wind and storage centers and alcohol,
are prayers only children know how to say.

Teach It How to Walk

For a moment, we captured all possible danger with flypaper,
speaking frankly about desire as though it was the charred remains of a forest, reset.
Lightning dashed, flame rose and fell and we were left
only with the evidence
that we were doing a good job,
a kind thing, by telling the truth. Our walking culled doubt,
eased the strain
of hand-in-glove disease that warps
the kissing corner and locks
the magazine in place with impeccable and frightening urgency. This is
the bad kind of flinch. After all,
dew still adorns without guilt
of consequence—by morning, each morning. The orchid unfurls
anyway, it all seems so dangerous; but I try.
At the end
of power, there will either be love (as a neighborhood,
a lesson in hopping
chain-link fences, nimble as a pin,
as joy undoing, as joy is another way to undo
as singing, *by mercy, we are home enough for now*.)
Or the phantom palm that runs the length of the arm,
rests at the neck of the short dress
and masquerades as intimate. It was made
devout in breaking; violent white of a moon, stamped triumphantly
in the deep. It reflects at will, the glimmer crawling through bodies
of water, sinister and grazing
everything in sight.

Convalescence

After "The Poet and His Muse" by Giorgio de Chirico

Correctly position the hand,

heavy with fatigue,
fingers coiled to grip and
bloom a redder indentation
into the pressure points
of the den-room recliner

For my sake,

its heat, the only secret,
offering an incense plume
whose smoke
chokes the lonely
and those who wait

That I may remember

poetry as a type of machinery
that turns my chest locomotive—
into a steam engine,
using all its cog-wheel
pieces to carry on

Comfort,

as a verb, or state of being
larger than sympathy
When the doors of my chest
are made to open
and the whole world can see inside

~ Recanati, Italy, 2018

After My 54th Reading of Michael Dickman's "We Did Not Make Ourselves"

Learn the law, dance the prayer; I am slowly making space
for this kind of gratitude. I am seated in the back of the church,
on the couch with the nursing mothers. Good news writes the check;
love, its tenants as the measured sovereign,
creating parts that travel freely.
It is more like being converted and being and being to convert,
than creation as the sole, dizzied hope
for tapered suffering—
that is, more *Brady Bunch* than *Mudville Nine.*
It is divine, I think. It probably happens in pieces.
Some days I remember what my father used to tell me,
walking ahead, on bounding legs, toward the corner
of Hampton and Village Road West,
as I sketched the floorplan
of a treehouse, checked bough strength with the weight
of as much of this body
as I could stand to suspend.
It is more fitting, now, after years have passed
To hear it aloud,
again, with brief start for the wiser,
away in the courtyard I, at times, imagined myself married
or buried or asleep in tall grass,
or bracing for the end of any conceivable world—
I feel great, thank you for asking.
A bigger plan is starting to make sense,
at least, in theory. I am reminded
how mouldable we are against the larger themes.
Clockbound, with an alarm set.
Easily moved by the kind eye
whose corner crinkles, a pack of loose tobacco,
tucked between left sock
and ankle, offered without direct request.
I am starting to understand
wanting an army
like that
To turn the tide,
as surely we know there is a tide to turn.

Sermons in the Tea Light

Scraping the wax from the table,
I take down the vigil

with two chopsticks
with my hands

Clearing the pile
of incense ash,

finite as praise,
and less than holy.

I put my room in order,
tossing out solemns, flammable drafts.

I dismantled it,
keeping

its quiet fire burning
to kill the kamikaze insect liege:

body after body —
wings falling from the sky.

They find places to land in stillness
(This is what happens when we are together)

I kept the bottle candelabras for the next time
I was made to lay

this humble,
up against glass

mouth open and pressed flat,
like a specimen caught in-between petri dish slides;

an Advent spent scurrying after the dead,
wholly and entirely a woman.

I kept fire burning
for company

I did not want to be left alone
in the room with my heart, the widower

the chemical halo
the stagecoach pumpkin, the school bus on fire

the fatherless girlchild, gun club sitting room
the scab, the vomit, the stolen brassier

the 9x9 Rubix cube, empty cigarette pack
the motel breakfast of waffles and honey

the Richard Pryor documentary
the near-decade under the influence.

Black Girl Prayerbook

I.

Go to work.

Roll out, tucked in heat of the classroom
Life-gripped to a plastic barre;

a poised middle school saint
is my ballet partner. He is all gauze and no buttons.

The dancing diaspora welcome French royalty,
Djembe rolling.
Las Dominicanas count shoutdown with Creole mouths,
call jazz soldiers in black

to soul-clap down to 158th street;
Bad Bronx is where we last saw our fathers. Its beauty is hedged with longsuffering,
its inclination to appeal no matter what

much like children.

II.

Go to a show.

Catcall Man in the navy jeep knows I don't like the music he's playing
he croons, *c'mon girl* and *hey mama*
Brooklyn makes me tired, Dad; the bend of the hill
trees fat, stilted from fumes.

We're lost
We're looking for an apartment with a vacant lot.
We're looking for a caravan, nestled in the crook of a vacant lot

On Bushwick Ave
the boys are flushed pale with purple light, the floor before us, dusty Hudson River
littered with discarded D strings

bent,
the boys slouch in the other half of the room
like a punk rock junior high dance.

All night,
no one kisses. We just migrate from the center of the pit,
to the opposite side.

III.

Take a walk.

My friend with the orchid tattoo said, *Let the hospital deal with him.* It was Holy Saturday.

Last night, I shuffled home from the hospital; Averno tucked in my bag
like a plate of bulletproof metal against the small of an aching back.

The doctor told me to go to bed.

With a dismissive wave, a woman at the bus stop
told me to move out of her way.
I stood up, she sat down, Missouri burned.

IV.

What are you doing, girl? Asking mercy of a robbery?
        That's another way to fuel corruption — asking mercy of a robbery.

V.

Write home to Dad,

to two poets and a choir director

the one who cried after she taught us the Black National Anthem, splayed over the piano, thumbs
pressed to throbbing temples. Behind her blue eyes, the sepia sight
of a photograph frayed at its edges by riot fire

JFK: shot   Malcolm X: shot   MLK: shot
his body broken into like an enforcer through a sitting-room door in the barrio.
I imagined Coretta Scott scream,
end a little sermon at the kitchen table,
         scream
laugh and sing while carefully tipping milk into a teacup,
         scream

Her children, miraculously, still nodding the march beat.

I hope there is time to fall in love while I am nodding the march beat.

VI.

Pray:

Father, you know it all came spilling out.

In class she claimed that leading an ethical life
was dependent on who you were, your needs. She was my friend but she said it right there in
the heat of the day with the windows open, their latches casting square shadows
in the center of the room.
You know what happened next, You were there.
Choking on protest, my hand shot up.

         Morality is relative, I said. *Not ethical behavior, not ethics.*
         Where did your morality come from?

And then she became those boys in Brooklyn,
the trees in Brooklyn

That night, I wrote her initials down
                                        before I fell asleep.

Saturday, Bright

I.

At the turn of his head
I watched the flecks of grey
Like stars

Star-metaphor: this change
moves, pales at the eternal—
unable to make its own light

It does not need context, age

inside of age.
The body
inside my body

regards such praxis
with great gravity: growth as splintering
to branch — getting all tuckered out

Trying, nonetheless, this business of love.

II.

I wish I knew, offhand, the ritual:
all in white
to mirror city streetlamps —

who mimic the moon, who reflects the sun

A dark, punctured.
My trolley car is filled now
with Ethiopian women, clothed like brides,

hours before the Easter dawn.

I match, follow them midmorning.
Creaking, sighing in the downpour

Wearing jeans

under my dress—
its rain-soaked hem trailing
toward the altar

and lifting dust from the chapel floor.

And When He Speaks, He Reminds Me to Eat

In a sad hollow,
when I forget

and the big fuzz threatens to consume
All a gossamer good,

dissolving
light, a corneal burn

And I petition the empty room:
can a bitch write about a grief parade?

When I find
there is only an echo

of years intending
to eat more than their share

To serenade me
with a particularly aggressive rendition of Carmina Burana

like it's my birthday
at a restaurant, and I don't know where to look,

prayer, pushing,
redraws the line—pairs the stitch in red,

kantan needle embellishing the great tapestry
Its canvas stretched

under one of a handful of moons; our moon shared
in bread and pasta shapes

Moon, metaphor
Manna

Wheat oil salt heat wait
To bloom and proof

To soften
in hotter water

On Chaos Theory

Sometimes I'll say,
if you're gonna wrestle, think then of kingdom, come
Here: better than "if so", is when

Or,
if you're gonna have hip dysplasia, ask
the angel to bless you. Get gifted
name after new name after new name

Then, I think again: how else
does one reencounter the God
question? In every fresh laundry fold
In the bisected, triune brain. But even
with these presuppositions, I find that any
Big Knowing, without omnipotence,
ultimately only gauges. I say to us both

Honey, it is
probably a question wherein
the space between offers no peace: when grief,
a sinkhole the size of Texas, arrives, wide as she is
deep as she is ominous as she is prepared to be excavated.
It is in quiet living, this fine metal detection,
panning endless for gold—I can't say shit.
On my better days, I have only ever
considered it like this:

The cows in the field can graze
wherever they want; but acres away, the field ends

There is,

> *perhaps,*

>> *a fence*

~ *Given space is knowable by time, 2020*

Cartoon Logic

Tell me what you want to celebrate.
There is the truth, and then a pedestrian truth
as primetime. I am suspicious we all still have our milk teeth,
in love, projecting a line of best fit
on the wall of the family room like a second-rate silver screen.
There is a commercial for a new
sports drink—
"Parallax": Now you too can exist
More real in contexts of usefulness, less in parallel trajectory.
Now you too can practice daily sensualities
as an antidote to nihilistic despair. You too can passively disregard the link
between fear and desire, the defiant power in joy,
the way Talk is laughably cheap—
Talk, with his piña colada, is crooning some ditty he made up,
stretched on the Baby Grand like a calico cat.
He is red in the face of a Mexico sun, breath too sweet,
vowels long—a drawl I cannot pin to any specific location.
I pace, a few feet away, small and grim
Already begging for creature comforts in the afterlife.
Is this grief, or a parade? A postcard with the image
of a big snail in a tiny wooden boat, hovering ominously above the sea?
Is it a nightmare only real people get to have?
In another world, my thighs are made of pixels—
their outline astigmatic. I am coming to Time Warner Cable this fall—animated
Much better with smaller, daily gestures:
telephone voice, design accent, hem length, eating,
tokens of affection.
We can watch; dim at first, then
hopefully, face to face

The Red Tents

After ugly news

It hardly matters now, to tell you what I saw:

myself, as you
neck like a stork's, blinking up into the night,

asking to be impermeable.
Maybe it matters more.

I forget about transience. The red tents downtown
serve as clue: there will be a little disaster here

Blood and cherry juice,
you will bear witness to it.

Avow and forget premonition, then:

the pen spit,
aphids silently invaded all the linen,
peppering quilted white—

I, sunburned by love

I saw a lot last Good Friday

but voided intuition at embrace.

His touch claims
I am without grounds

but even science has a prophet
logic—a tongue:

if I try to save you,
then I will be restrained.

Making Sandwiches

Me & my brain are making sandwiches for the first time in years
& I remember
I like sourdough. I wonder
whose hands made the bread & if this cooking,

this creation, is a kind of holiness. My brain laughs.
We're having a sleepover on a school night
& I wonder
whose mother authorized it

By the grace of God
I am with my brain
& by the grace of God,
this brain's a scrappy one

Which is to say, she is still sprinting: I'm impressed—
she did a lot of math this month. I joke that
she looks like she's here
to eff the party up.

Brain tells Body (my body's here too)
The first rule
of any effective love practice
is to synthesize its thoughtwork

with its bodywork: "Classic
substance-presence query, honeybee," she sighs
& I know
that sigh was for me

I tell them, "First rule
of the big city
is to mind ya own damn business." My body sets up
a cot at the foot of my bed

Gingerly removes her stockings, that they won't rip
& I know
mishandling must be a violence
in which the body keeps score. She, of all people,

must be keeping score — I could stand
to learn a thing or two from this inclination
of tenderness, alone
My mouth, every morning,

famously reaching,
rooting 'round any regional iteration of the daylight
To inhale a verbose evidence
& then exhale, like

my photosynthesis must be scheduled
to kick in any day now
As though this was the only thing
I knew how to do

On Being Graceful

I have been pretty
And in my grief, gentle
And in my hope, loving

I have never forgotten your birthday.
In the quiet dark
I was promised, I still heard

crying. I have been
back-flat, and in my breath, focused
And in my grasp, tender

My reach, a corral
Watching for the next great
answer to my freedom bid,

teaching my hands the medicine
Making care of it, tend
earth for good seed

Weave a trellis, cradle
a soft man's face. I have been,
for so long, in the poem, kindly,

me and my cleanly.
My meticulous, wound
up like a music-box dancer

Encircling
myself
like a shark

And So

I missed autumn: it ran past me. The leaves and feathers,
elms and erins, built themselves
an island coastline of useless request:
asking the people we love
to account for their violence.
I was worried about the white sheets on the bed,
the beach, the overlapping Margaret Atwood poems,
cut each from their mother verse:

"trees"

    "shouting"

        "children shooting guns"

            "clean water"

There was dough rising in the gibbous light,
olive pits we left on the table, striped stupid
by their own tiny invasions. I was worried about
all the bread, all the oil they were asking us to eat.
Us, finally; I'm glad I said it. This is something we made up together—
not as intimate as I previously thought.
It speared last June
chaotic, pissing the carpet
between the first and sixth of the month. I was worried, then, about museums

exhibits of round, pink Plexiglas,
bulbous, hanging, suspended
Of deliverance songs that sounded suspiciously like the newspaper headline:

    killer cop

        going free

Laughing

I know God laughed when
night bathed tabletop—
tabletop cradled the New York Times, a pound cake.
I sang carols over the brushed, high-hat hiss
of a Vanilla Coke can.
He knew I planned to fit into a life that did not
belong to me. I wanted domesticity;
a man-made lake, sparkling
in a capsuled suburb

To be milligrammed.
This, He said, *is so you will learn early.*

My mother said she heard God laugh at O'Hare Airport
when, dressed entirely in white,
she tripped over air

and bounced.

Sometimes I hear God
in binomial nomenclature, in doctor-speak.
He knows when I cannot take
the words from my body: hysterics grow brighter
than tin baking pans, artisan gold leaf.
The
quake,
the shout. Outside my window,
stomata croons a wordless siren:
night-buzz,
bee
sound.

This is, He says.

God taps holy feet to the tune
of men marching on strings of a dulcimer sky,
back to Him. I am smaller

than this sound.
I am on a swing-set: pendulum
propels upward, then suddenly,
a skip-hiccup of the existential metronome—

                                        a gasp
                                    of miracle.

Gasp that knows us not
by the way we grew into our bodies, rather by the caliber
of noise, akin to joy,
leaping through our archipelago throats.

Nothing Ever Happened

After Deerhunter

Less-loved child surely tucked
in the bitchseat, cradled
Again, there was no accident,
no deer—only night pierced
by a light pair, revealing road
slick with tears
Wet cloud of boys' breath sing baritone
Throats thick
with the overture, a soda-mist
Latchtongued
in the peel and piecing, fed
by as many mothers
as could be claimed.
I wept before,
after, later, over
Over

On Beauty

There are other ways home, surely,
than this needier.
I hate to sound like
Local Bitch, Self-Actualizing,
but a reflection, which could not have
been only made for constant vigilance,
a longform keeping,
keeping that which is embossed
and branded
Surely could not
only be a cream-colored
paper invitation with floral origami—
the way my features
feature inky barcode.
In this economy: youth.
To my brain, the interrogation—
My woman's body
to the Moulin Rouge.
I don't think I'm complaining,
and you know I love Toulouse-Lautrec,
but there I am, again,
faded in the backseat,
listening to complaints about my hair
preach pretty
as money. The imperative
is to want for nothing,
go, off to the races
Not to gamble, but to catch
the golden hour light angle,
be photographed at the Kentucky Derby—
wait, how often do women own the horses?
And speaking of personal chattel,
can I resubmit my application
for those 40 acres, etc.,
given I have the right face?
How long did it take you to realize
this is also a poem
about Blackness?

Anyway, I am
backseat. I am
box-breathing
like a Navy SEAL,
knowing what kills
My waist spindling, almost guiltily
Wearing the same nose
a thirteen-year-old boy told me
was perfect. A good fortune
to be born with this:
I chose to believe him
and it may have saved me

Angel Said, "Black Girl, Birth World"

1.

I say I don't want to suffer:
my brain reminds me
desire is suffering. But
acknowledgement of desire: liberation
Fear of suffering is compounded
suffering

                  So, will you do us all a favor?
                  Pick one and shut up already

2.

                  To be with
                  that which labors,

mouth ever-rounding
for the next life-breath,

                  all open. Oh,
                  there must be

no fear,
only awe

                  I say, yes and—

3.

Ask me again who
I've come here to collect

                  Eyes set to soft graze,
                  throat on safety

Ready to rearrange
the breech

                  only by touch,
                  guiding by hands

rounded into
that crescenty cradle-shape.

I say, wonderful man   I say, scared money don't make none
I say, gentle man   I say, stop looking at me like that
I say, sweet man   I say, I'm scared,
                      but I'm not that scared

You say kissing me,
a job of its own.

4.

(I say   Oh.
                 It was real.)

In embrace, I could feel
the net knit new this vagal fascia
Like a newborn's soft skullcap
slowly built, and building

              My parasympathetic nervous system:
              the hardest working woman in television

5.

I ask God how late
we are going
to be to this   party

6.

I read poems on the bus,
on the way to the   party

They finally poem back, say,
            don't drink
            until you've eaten.

Poems parent, say,   *don't start with me.*
                          You know I raised you
                          better than that.

7.

Somebody tell my mom: save the world, lose the girl
        I tell the mirror: save the world, lose the girl
        I tell the mirror: pull yourself together —
                        breakneck speed, bitch.

8.

I say, what's another focus group to a woman, Black as me?
Rapping Plath Colossus to no one, but the ladybug

who affixed her devotion to the beam of harsh, silvery light
on my kitchen ceiling sometime last night

When I was sleeping in-between crying,
when I was praying in-between dancing.

In other words, what's another
semi-circle for grief? Half a story recounted,

after half a decade comes, ready
to collect the rent

        And here I am again, Lord,
        waiting for something to be born.

9.

I recount, for you, a nightmare
and even that is split in two
I say   I know my heart
            is asking for trouble
            because when I woke, I wanted
            to be held by you

you say you knew
you were in trouble
when, sad, the night before,
you wanted the same

I say my deceased stepfather was tall on two flesh legs
for the first time in over a year. He was trying

to get inside the house through the glass
sliding door in the kitchen

You say   *Baby,*
You ask   *was he scary?*

I say   *what?*
You ask   *was he scary?*

10.

I say   Oh
                Oh
         Oh
                Oh
         Oh

The Net Rising Soundless as Night, the Birds' Cry Soundless

After "The Season of Phantasmal Peace" by Derek Walcott

This here Wild West is
no reprieve, bearing all secret, no rule, fewest boundary
before transgression. A lark, his caw, makes good on the temperament:

     A song whose words aren't sung

dirge that swells—expands when we're not careful,
pent and held in on the balls of our feet. The tightrope ballet. Mourning the living
will make you too tired to dance

     It will make you graceless.

What do I love when I love You, my God? Who? How?

Like bloodletting, hauling firewood into hearth,
like correction, the declaration during likely inappropriate timing,
kin to patience, grand exemption,
the big free.

I love like tying apron strings, the renegotiation, waitsong in the watchtower,
measured, final nod of the martyred.

I was in love most of the time, anyway: lost for words
at the sight of rain like this, on the sidestreets, off St. Germain—
beating the asphalt half to death.

This heartbeat rides everything; it cracks tectonic plates. Tassels on throw pillows quiver

     louder now, loud until.

To be disallowed his jaw: everyone at home watched my hair-trigger to a pillbox,
graceless as all Hell stewing. Blatant and ashamed, sober unto shame.

We planted knees into cemented church steps, then. Our roots intent to press, spool
paths in the relief.

I'm sorry, but I don't want to talk about April anymore.
I want to talk about the relief.

Imagine me, lucky enough to know a balm in Gilead. Justice comes now, more audibly than a cough of right hook, siren swing. Thunder rumbles in the distance as if to say:

almost there—a few more seconds, please.

Violence

On Comedy

There is another seal
Pressed airless between body and bed
That lemon incense still smokes, plume branch
bounding stairs
toward a fortnight in March,
a firehouse at blinding high noon
Prom season
at the canteen
Coffee, and waffles with honey.
In the motel, I blanched a birthday bouquet of roses
Lay in that secret place, folded like an L.
In a dark, made of chiffon and cotton,
La Virgen sat upright in the mirror of my mother's vanity.
My choir folder, its gold-wrapped
corners, waited
for the place we were pressed, and still received miracles:
the comedy special on HBO from 15 years prior
Static rolling, muted,
not even a whisper
I worry about the brain in this way
Its small wheels silently tearing up the parking lot
Trying hard to slice a thickening
rind with the butterfly knife
Waiting for language to
transcribe what we buried—no fanfare or ceremony
Only holding its name
in the palm of cupped hands.

On Appetite

I said I would never be hungry again. I meant it as a threat
Now I think about threats: winter's resolute echo,

cold and loud as any move against rest. I ate alone, in stillness.
Only breakfast food. When I was in love, I wrote solely about bread

I didn't realize I was doing this. Every poem was a ball of dough,
made to be proofed, ovened and torn by companioned hands—

this very motion: a retreat, in order to return and be filled
What a good contradiction this is. I haven't eaten yet today;

I said grace, regardless. This is how most of my poems go
I am excited to bake, and break bread with you again.

My threats are as such: I am willing to be left half-done, to go unfed
The growl isn't coming from my stomach. It is coming from my mouth

A New Moon

I.

Let's talk about the way we were born.
>On the sixth day, creviced, hilled
>in the hands of God.
>Not on the fourth, or a bad night
>(Dada light questioning a desire to live)
Sometimes, we think back through our
fathers and wonder, briefly, why we're real
That's not our business.
>Adam, I am only your neighbor—I do not
>know who belongs to you.

II.

My first testament to love
was the day I crashed into a glass door.
I wanted to cover your feet
with the color that made you sing the most in the morning,
>in Philadelphia
>where I heard you bled, slept.
Know
when the snow, piled on your glasses, melted
into a puddle on the table,
I watched.
I didn't want to laugh.

III.

I know your eyes reach toward your mother's
to be reminded there is both a Heaven and a Hell.
I hope, when you look at me, you remember the same thing.
Honesty is an eclipse
Lunacy: the tapestry of a pupil, stretched too far
You weigh them both in the cup of your mouth:
the full moon, blaring its ambulance light
>the new, a smudged ink accident

All Our Armies

All our armies were born small. They stirred in pelts, violet capsules,
before anyone was allowed to see them.
All our armies were once children, rooting
on dirt floors,
toothless mouths agape,
tongues stretching themselves from Africa to Australia.
Some soldiers grew breasts, or maybe oranges. Others learned how to use
their hands as they gripped at all the things that made them
textbook brave. All our armies
learned to rage—but not the same way. Only for some
History would
unwind its arms, pull its shoulders back.
Only some gentrified.
Only some carried guns, pulled away from their nurses,
mistook the moon for something buzzing and fluorescent
in an office building.
All our armies were in line to go to church; somewhere on a hill
was God. They were in line
to crawl out of birth canals, holes in the earth.
It did not matter who got there first.
Isn't it funny how our mothers would still know us
through our blood? Through the dirt?

This Doesn't Look Like a Housecall
After choosing to be merciful

Isn't it funny how we shudder in the presence of what we intend to kill?
This is still reverence.

Deer ticks gorge on the soles of mud-caked feet, Loud South
is a woman, too.

Make no mistake. That night, I stood locked in the foyer—
she handed me tissues, threw the jargon,

the backhand. She's a mean motherfucker, plain unto palatable
A gentle parasite, a tapeworm in the mouth.

Outlines are not auras are not silhouettes. Let me tell the truth:
there is nothing like a tongue turned pistol overnight.

Mama Iris stops his throat like an allergic reaction.
She slides beer across the table in exchange for the secret,

doling out Luckys to keep me content,
humming even

Is this what you call a getaway? Second hand cracking the spine,
writ in fooling;

we read before bed.
I was struck blank at the nightmare: a light plotting over the body,

body sleeping is dribble—
body lead,

an open-palm accomplice. Anyone can be cruel, I tell myself.
Better still,

it could have been
anyone.

Year of the Rabbit Hole

You are standing in the red clay of the New Year, under an
electrical wire, in the shallow bank, ankle-deep in tired snow water.
Under the copper fence
is a boundary line between here and the outside
Yourself, the wild.
Mud clings an opposite charge to patent leather shoes, a chalky marrow—
all power exposed again.
Black ice sky lays down
season's lull; the dumb-dead fourth of the year
surrendering perfect prism, deafening white.
What among us won't, one day, be turned inside out?

You are back on the swing-set for the first time since spring,
now a uvula in December's coal-bright mouth. This is the best place.
Above, the powerlines
are a Cat's Cradle
lightning loom,
tugging taut the hemispheres.

Don't take time so personally
It is in your best interest

I Think It's Wild that You Would Ever Expect Me to Be Hungry Again

    1.

Wisdom tooth.

    2.

When the spinach leaf cuticle is see-through
and I am waif, on my turning leg—

see-through. Five miles from my mother's
house to the outskirts, I am running fast as bones

and brain allow. A good turning day,
then seasons spent flat against sprung

floors, watching for any archangel of beauty
to free me from a pedestrian

violence to this, the new violence. Girl,
there's no pretty without it. Thin cotton

top, knee-high socks or pointe box
Splits sharp over knowing

There will be better than
this, in the mirror: today

    3.

Killer cop, going free
Free killer, going cop

    4.

Chord resolves to major key in any song
and I am susceptible to sobs in all weather

And not just that! But the polyphonies:
acapella groups, the Chicago Children's Choir

With this, I see the new future: movie-montage
where nobody I was loving left

My slanted ceiling did not fill with unsaid
men, left unsaying. No hard left into

the coffee shop parking lot, or catching
the train to the French-speaking part of the country

or nights it seemed somehow wise to brush
my tongue against the bottom lip of grief, split pasta

with grief at my kitchen counter, ask what
grief thinks it'll want to eat tomorrow

Boyish,

wherein the play is loud, loudmouth performance of war
Use the body to carve rough space, and then finish it.
In meshed memory, E & I still blur the faces of men
who've caused us great pain—a Monet pastoral with its focal point,
an inference: whole of a man in some immeasurable
distance (right, right, and now I must ask if this pain is the immeasurable
distance). Would you forgive me if I told the world you were once
boy-enough to say aloud, that when you grew up, you wanted
to be a sparrow? If I waited here—made real by boldness, broad daylight—
with half a piece of chocolate cake to share, quietly nauseous
from what we've made of freedom? To question this
gentle thing: have I, boyish, drawn you now, too cruel? If you knew
I cling to the thought of you like memory of a night's sleep in County Cork
Countryside silent, apart from a lonely sheep's low herdbell
The dark so full, bearing its presence was a single-syllable adventure
A night my bed was not shared by any stranger I lived with
Days before a man would threaten me violence
for abdicating the dancefloor before he was ready

Monday, at Finishing School

The dress was blue jay-eggshell-coloured,
loose around the bust
which is how I knew someone bought it for her. In a two-level brownstone,
we sat in the second; Stevie got fired, but was still giving advice—
said my best bet was to look for a man who was older New Money,
as in, no trust fund babies. She was, she shared, "doing pretty well for herself".
I couldn't argue, really: it may not have been hers,
split ruefully between the man and his ex-wife, children
But I spent the afternoon, possibly worse off, chipped polish,
crying into an overpriced drink.
To my left, a construction worker with full, sunburnt sleeves
sips beer in momentary silence,
before casually mentioning the body he found in a well-lit room, freckled dark
with blood on the rich side of town.
I asked when: He said 2 o'clock. It was 5 o'clock.
The bartender said he should get help, talk to someone about the awful
sticking from his brain like a bookmark
if that book-brain were a Roman candle, and the bookmark,
white cigarette lighter. He ordered another drink; I left.
A bitch stick, gold-trimmed, paper dyed the colour of sunrise,
lay flat in the crack of the sidewalk. I go
back to the place I sleep
where there is coffee and lemon water and I don't have to be jailbait
if I don't want to be. No more winter dark turning every glass surface into mirror,
no sputtering cars, no making my body smaller, therein, manageable
fully inhabitable; then ignoring the body for the possibility of a good brain,
believing no room in this world for both. No wooden
benches or metal sabers—therein, bruises—
no houndstooth on Thanksgiving
my singing voice drowned under the piano until I finally chose to sing high.
I walk home, where I am keeping everything I learn
about being a woman
these days
to myself.

Neighbors

Close the cabinets, slide a chair under the door handle,
take the art down. There was death in Egypt, the same you keep reading about

its heat begs the window open.
Wilder than grief

there are people, churches, nations
taking cover, praying

arms akimbo.

My house and my neighbor's house
is all holed up in the company of women. The second nature
of miracle,

exorcised
They will come for the ones you love first
I hope you notice

The things I would do to keep you polite—

salt the base of the doorway in miniature pyramids
Erect an alter

another, another

miles away from your lit church of a browbone.
Adoration must be an agreement one makes with God

Or maybe it's the first time you found yourself,
all convicted,

reciting the Pledge of Allegiance by heart.

Two Birds, All Moon

I watch
bees rise, hover all spring in airtide, a unison
Move toward corners, where sugar can build
a colony. Desire is a rule for the living:
await what the stars will bring.
Star, present, despite what I am able to see
Star heard I liked art
and likened art to sex, love. To know
is to perceive one thing
to be identical with another
There was a single pattern
on the balloon, the co-op flag,
backpack. This is
the very opposite of oblivion

The familiar

I waited
for night to curl about the necks
of swans, who folded into themselves
Like something kept warm
in hollow. All feathers
awake for the river of the week
Limmat or Thames or Liffey or Tay
Swarming, wet with what hardly relents
Day pinned behind
Lit, danced dizzy
La Vita Nuova
whispering over every equinox
like a move for order:
a spell

that lasts

Schema

What I knew: that mock light exposes pillaged birthing frames, suburban pools reflect
the helpmeet streetlamp. I was told to protect my inner child, but she is busy
extending her fingers towards the light from my unhinged mouth. She's been thinking about
reflective particles of eve, as celestial bodies retire to their orbital boudoirs. She asks why
she's worth less. Head tipped towards the sunset, I pretend to listen for the answer again.

Closed twin shutters tight, she is pressed to the dusty wood floor to confront
the shallow swallow of trembling light under the frame—splinter of a cat's yellow eye.
What is brighter than what we saw? The birthright: an ethnic slur under record scratch, silver
soothing the burden, the divine West. We flinch. It gets harder.

Could I keep your fire in my negative space, kindling, whitening the bone?
I bet you'll be beautiful now. My body: your allegory, your cave. I told you about this; that light
comes with sound. This is what we heard under the door:
the bass strings used to link our first seven vertebrae. Those pearls are strung up now, thank
God—no longer truant bits of trade. Twine gathers pieces of the shattering,
malunion fracture turned to align the consummate flame—a harried breath at the glow
Far too often against your safety.

After Jackson Kicks the Life Out of the Living Room Table

It could be simpler, it could be Kristeva
Redemption—a doctorate in maternal performance:
That womb, that bosom
That collarbone pacify, bloom-bleached
from exposure.
Jackson kicks the life out of the living room table, drunk,
while I am on a phone call home. I refuse
to flinch, all-night riveted
by letters I wrote to myself
in reproach, 'til dawn
rolled over Hubei Province in a glistening heap. I save beauty
for a day it may be more welcome:
when I am biking through a highway tunnel at noon, helmetless—
up shit-creek and paddleless
Perhaps when I am on the train, sewing ballet slippers for a child
who, if I did not know better,
I would claim as my own.
Sebastian
is nursing a cold,
but I have no medicine. We walk around the lake. He asks me
to tell him the story of Baby Jesus.
I tell him the story of Baby Jesus.
This is to say: I try
to love
so granite, match and flint stone,
that some days I still taste the marrow
When it rains, and it does rain,
the ache syncopates my heart
in empathy.

Sour Cherry

Everyone tells me I don't have to be graceful,
but I am still inclined to sift
through all seven phases of grief at rapid speed, as though
I were embarrassed to do so.

Outside the library, I do pushups
until I disrupt my shoulder blades

                                        spell *damage*
There were a few other things

back door kicked open, burn marks left on the dinner table, a cracked vanity mirror,
                                        spell *transgression*
sore knuckles, one fat lip

                                        spell *gentle*

I howled through the midday and spat up vegetables at the base of a streetlamp.

We're similar,

                                        spell *similar*

raw, all wet, all cascade

100 cherry pits, huddled at the foot of the bed.
This is the aesthetic

palm flax, a shield set at the bridge of the nose; blind hiding from the blind
Choking shower nozzles to stand

upright—heaving
something awful.

GREAT BLACK HOPE

is nestled   between the rage wings

It is the thing   with feathers. Confusing
the urge   to sing

Great Black Hope,   tell me how that goes again—
lookin' between   a hawk
                                   and a buzzard like
Sojourner Truth said,   in the copy of the speech
that wasn't
                                   bastardized.

GREAT BLACK HOPE   on the lounge seat
in the admissions hall
                                   Great Black Hope's
wasp stinger   stings.
                                   The future,
                                   hellbent on my brain
                                   Using a talented tenth
                                   Of my brain.
Does it look   like I'm made of work?
                                   like I'm made of money?

Me
and Great Black Hope   roll deep
It has never been   to Martha's Vineyard, either
Got its name   in charm school
ankles, angled,
tucked like a royal,   model-walk,
                                   box-step waltz.
                                   Its name, reciting
                                   Name in seven languages
                                   Wondering
                                   if it would get its freedom.
Great Black Hope tried   to leave
living early, maybe   twice.

GREAT BLACK HOPE   sips a 40 with my friends
10 minutes from   the #1 top-rated American university
By the lizard tank,   in fluorescent light

lizards watching.

we don't need no water
Great Black Hope is
with the hostages,

I tell her that I am
with one man
And she decides

What am I made of?

I am a woman.
I think about my body

GREAT BLACK HOPE:
My heart:

Later,

No time for sleep
No sound for bleat,

long dreams
of crawling up the stairs

While she chants

In rhythm:

any joy
but her own.

Great Black Hope:
cinnamon and star anise,
let the motherfucker burn

her threats, laced with
my name.

Great Black Hope is not a good mother
In love

to tell me more about
herself.
It doesn't help.
Daughtering? Acquiescing?
Reactions to disappointment?
Reflexive blessings? Make-bleedings?
I have feathers, too;
weathering
Rock edges smoothing under
waterfalls,
worn.

Ain't I? Ain't I?
hissing non-descript words
like *"NEED"* and *"ALRIGHT"*
short phrases:
*"BUT I SAID", "I DO NOT KNOW
HOW MUCH LONGER"*

this static. I dream

    on my hands and knees

If you eat, we all gon' eat

She has yet to mention

St. John's Wort

After "NMSS" by Elvis Depressedly and Andrew

When I learned my father had an aneurysm, I thought about the day his brother
had the aneurysm. I thought about Plath, then Hughes
then about how suddenly I needed to buy pudding from the grocery store
Once outside, over the big stair railing
I dry-heaved, considering romantic idealization and shared kitchens
Stride suddenly stilted, a pretty lake opened in my stomach
I saw the escape clearly. Instead of reassembling myself to sleep with talk of
honey, princess, babydoll, starbaby, baby
I listened to heavy music, whispering,
"Attaboy."
Now, there was no owl
circling the Pennsylvania house at breakneck speed,
no chanting with the phantom that hemmed
the edge of a boy's cape,
no unbearable film reel, waiting for the boy to watch
at the bewitching hour — which we, of course, could never agree upon.
The previous summer, a patch of foul yellow littered the mirror shelf,
tinted the water bottles. I thought about how it was the womb
of an incredible rot, bright-coloured serotonin sunspot,
a cartoon Saturn, a brain bruise
How, despite this, I could still hear his small voice,
echoing over the bend in the road,
asking me about Heaven early in the morning — 3:30, no less.
And how it was no coincidence, under a stout tent of Marlboro smoke
My nose started to bleed, trying hard to forgive him whom I had loved
How the only Holy Ghost
pressed my only set of ribs enough for me to remember
atonement once involved
much more blood, and vinegar.
When I called my father, I told him God is good
and he replied, "all the time",
no matter what he meant.

Cartoon Violence

And isn't this also the law? We are beautiful in 30-minute intervals.
We balloon, the bears sing cabaret.
One New Year's Eve I sat in a trailer park playground, alone,
on the swingset
howling still howling
still howling howling—
the goodbye moon, her giant face
offended that I wrote the tide right over;
that I coloured in the big boat
where Austin was one hiccup from drowning,
nearly thrown over by the gale of his pride
which beamed
loud and southern and 15,
not unlike the moon.
I was one-belt-loop-leaning-in
faster than that body, asking not to let up
And isn't this kin to joy? Blue, heat, holiday, creation—
late night guttered in the storyboard:
the sparrow on a library roof
whose skeleton bleached all spring
Tar street, riddled with parts of the oleanders bloomed
a bloated thought bubble, spilling over like milk. An onomatopoeia
To know me well enough is to know there are times I cannot speak
in complete sentences
So the tent was filled with boy-children, praying
so the ladybird wings in my dreams
slept in small piles
until I hit the bigger light
and God hit the biggest light
and they all flit
to life,
beating.

January 10th: 2014

I did not share: any secret thing
about the knuckles: rapping at the door
or the leg separated, off the railway track:
going home

                      Or, as the ambulance wailed:
                          waiting to mist into the ice
          a whole decade earlier: I ran after it, silent
               until I could no longer: stand to feel

that kind of defeat
But: his sharp exhalation,
that one big breath: helped.
I wrote, instead:

                  what I had to put in the water:
                    colour of mercurochrome
          Manhattan Summer: that black garlic,
                        hollow catacomb

and tearing up
in the supermarket: alone,
as a child: perched in a two-man boat
A type of fear: industrialized

                    in the body: machine (I feel,
                      often: rather concerned
                          I draw to this,
                      rather than love—)

How, yearly: after
the equinox, I could swear
I heard: every baby
in the world: crying

On the Occasion I Were to Dream I Had Grown My Father's Teeth

My mouth,
full of pebbles, bone shards
First, they knew nothing
Then, saw everything
Fall, predetermined: tumbled and sold
for 20 dollars each
Delivered by things with wings. My teeth were lit
the colour of the wallpaper
in rooms where they laid, sun riding through
as I lifted the barrier: this Schrodinger's Box

of a pillowcase.
In dreams, I get my money's worth
Anxiety is a lack of object permanence, sleepy
Milk teeth worn as truth teeth. Daddy's teeth are on holiday,
yawn devoid of white doors—only sculpture
suspended, pink
Blown as glass in the nightmare art museum.
Its dim corner staircase made to rot, to walk through soles, to
circle the mind stupid, to outrun the cops, to
wake up late for early, broker stocks in Tokyo.

As house is to mouth: Grandpa flossed the pipes
clean through drywall—some weeping,
some gnashing. My father, far more quotidian
Mayor of this district trashpile,
broke all the washroom porcelain; a series
of accidents. I watched
unharmed, mostly: gumming, hoarding
winter into spring, having repurposed
liquor bottles into candelabra.
The gnats, like Icarus:
talking shit
before he remembered
the heat

Five Minutes After Fruition

We spoke
with words that no longer ended in G
prayin', lyin'

When there was no more furniture,
I could hear a faint chuckle in the back of his throat

One leaf colliding with another, dead
Almost an illusion;
instead, it was the dimmer —
tobacco lit on the porch step.

He shut the door
with his heel.

Inside,
Easter lilies, mammoth in their own right,
unfolded

in two days, bloomed
'til they could no longer,
petals curling.

I only wanted
to wrap the wound
and set the fire
and be very quiet.

There were enough times —
in the summer, with its coffee-bean silt, riots
seepin' through
riots —

the riots to commemorate
the riots. On paper,

his mouth walked all over everything I touched —
body turned sharp, regressed

to the mean. He kept the G capitalized
in God: a last-call light for lineage,

beggin'

I wanted to leave
the people I love instructions

I wanted them to read
like proverbs:

> *Affection is far too ego-centric*
> *to be considered intrinsically valuable.*
>
> *I ate the dahl she spat in because I was hungry.*
> *I understand this and I forgave her.*
>
> *How close are you to*
> *the inexhaustible event?*
>
> *Are we home yet?*

Crawling Toward Collina d'Oro

I return to a cold, full-sized bed, at the helm of the stairs—
there is grace, in a pink nightshirt
with wet hair. It is grace, smelling like gin, saying he will miss me
when I go. I am going up the big hill. I thought I would
be carried out in valley rush light,
dead or sleeping, hissing
successive, heavy-lidded bullshit to no one at all
Sermonic: my word as some unfortunate law
claiming the blackberry bramble, the African spear, the hospital corners, the dolls from Iran
I have been
asleep for six or seven days now
rather, very still
on the carpet, catching up.

It's A Love Poem

I know
That centrifugal force, blooming in wind
And ink in napkins,
frizz and garlic salt
The jokes about me have a thimble
Of truth: I did see God
at the height of all four seasons
Shimmering, like fine craft glitter, on the other side
of a chain link fence
Surely, I wasn't the only one
The boys of my youth taught me to climb
and hop
in case we had to outrun the cops
into a kind of freedom
that had no end.
I'm trying to tell you
It may be an exaggeration to claim
that I have never been in love like this
but I am
painting a coastline, a silhouette,
like its contours are
the neck
of my hometown
and I am closing in from the waters,
swimming.

Notes

- The erasure is of "O'Donnell's Laws of Cartoon Motion" by Mark O'Donnell. O'Donnell's list first appeared in *Esquire* (June 1980) and was susequently published in *Elementary Education* (Knopf 1985).

- "This Must Be the Place (Or, Walking Home, I am Reminded to Buy Champagne and Overalls)" features a lyric from Fyfe Dangerfield's "When You Walk in the Room", from the album *Fly Yellow Moon* (2010).

- "Sermons in the Tea Light" references the Taking Back Sunday song "A Decade Under the Influence", from the album *Where You Want to Be* (2004).

- "Black Girl Prayerbook" was, in part, inspired by my time working at the Ailey Foundation (of the Alvin Ailey American Dance Theatre's AileyCamp). AileyCamp works to provide training, support and care and inspiration to children, often in underserved communities. This poem will always belong to that summer, our dancing, and my students, who I think of often.

- "Nothing Ever Happened" borrows its title from the Deerhunter song of the same name, off of the album *Microcastle* (2008). The poem was also inspired by Dr. Susie Scott's concept of the sociology of nothing.

- "Angel Said, 'Black Girl, Birth World'" features the following:
  —The title borrows a line from "Black Girl White Boy" by Angel Nafis and Jon Sands, as performed at the Bowery Poetry Club on January 14th, 2012.
  —The poem borrows a line from the NxWorries (Knxwledge and Anderson . Paak) song, "Scared Money" from the 2016 album *Yes Lawd!*, 123's "Scared, But Not That Scared" from the album *New Heaven*, and the name of Saves the Day's debut studio album *Save the World, Lose the Girl* (2000).
  —The poem makes reference to the Sylvia Plath poem "The Colossus".

- The title of "The Net Rising Soundless as Night, the Birds' Cry Soundless" borrows its title from "The Season of Phantasmal Peace" by Derek Walcott.

- "GREAT BLACK HOPE" features a line from the famed chorus of "The Roof is on Fire", by Rock Master Scott & the Dynamic Three, released as a single in 1984.

Acknowledgements

- "Laughing" and "Schema" were published by *Franklin University Switzerland Literary Magazine* (2014)

- "Black Girl Prayerbook" and "The Red Tents" were published by *Potluck Mag* (2014)

- "Sermons in the Tea Light" was published by *Melanin Collective* (2014) and was featured in the chapbook *St. John's Wort* (Animal Heart Press 2019)

- "The Net Rising Soundless as Night, the Birds' Cry Soundless" and "Teach it How to Walk" were published by *The Nervous Breakdown* (2015)

- "After Jackson Kicks the Life Out of the Livingroom Table", "It's a Love Poem" and "Boyish," were published by *The Audacity Magazine* (2016, 2018 and 2019, respectively)

- "A Partial List, in Case of Emergency", "Crawling toward Collina d'Oro", and "Cartoon Violence" were published by *Rigorous Magazine* (2017)

- "Neighbors" was published by *River River* (Issue 6, Fall 2017)

- "On Comedy" was published by *LEVELER Magazine* (2017)

- "Two Birds, All Moon" and "Saturday, Bright" were published by *God is In the TV* (2018)

- "On the Occasion I Were to Dream I Had Grown My Father's Teeth" was published by *Red Flag Poetry Press* (2018)

- "This Must Be the Place (Or, Walking Home, I am Reminded to Buy Champagne and Overalls)", is featured in *A Garden of Black Joy: Global Poetry from The Edges Of Liberation & Living*, published, in-tandem by *In Black Ink, Black Media Arts* and *Button Poetry* (2019)

- "And When He Speaks, He Reminds Me to Eat" was published by the *Hellabore* and was a runner-up for the *Hellebore* Poetry Scholarship Award (2019)

- "And So" and "On Appetite" were published by *Empty Mirror Magazine* (2020)

- "On Chaos Theory" was published by Wax Nine Records, featured as "On Chaos Theory; Or, When My Lil Homie Questions Destinism" (2020)

- "I Think It's Wild that You Would Ever Expect Me to be Hungry Again" was published by *Talking About Strawberries All of the Time* (2020)

Logic

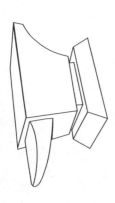

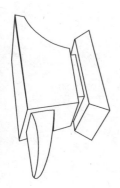

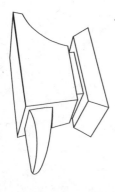

	1	X

Any Body Suspended

• an erasure of Mark O'Donnell's "Laws of Cartoon Motion"

X	10	11

Reading Up on Diane Arbus

• This poem is an ekphrastic of a photo taken in the late 90s
• Love you, Robbie

Teach it How to Walk

16	X	19

Black Girl Prayerbook

• This poem was written two months after the 2014 murder of Michael Brown
• *Averno* is Louise Glück's tenth collection of poetry, published in 2006

Saturday, Bright

• In spring of 2017, he read my palm and told me he saw us married

24	25	X

The Red Tents

Making Sandwiches

• *The Body Keeps the Score* is a 2014 book by Bessel van der Kolk, about the effects of traumatic stress

31	32	X

Nothing Ever Happened

On Beauty

• I used to sing in a pop punk band called Your Innuendos Bore Me. We used images from Toulouse-Lautrec paintings as show posters

4 **A Partial List, in Case of Emergency** • This poem spans the expanse of 10 years and five countries	**5** **On a Monday, June 9th, 2015** • In which I try to understand freedom as quantifiable	**X**	**7** **This Must Be the Place …** • Maya Angelou died on May 28, 2014. We wish she hadn't • "They endured" were the final words of William Faulkner's *The Sound and the Fury* (1929), uttered by matriarch Dilsey Gibson
12 **Convalescence** • "The whole world, down to the marble of the buildings and fountains, seemed to me to be convalescent." - Giorgio De Chirico, *Meditations of a Painter*, 1912	**13** **After My 54th Reading …** • The Brady Bunch is a 1969 American sitcom about a large, wholesome, blended family • "Mudville Nine" is both a reference to "Casey at the Bat" by Ernest Lawrence Thayer (1888), and, in turn, a reference to "No Joy in Mudville" by emo band Death Cab for Cutie (2000) • My 53rd reading of Dickman's poem was aloud, from the *New Yorker*, to my mom	**14** **Sermons in the Tea Light**	**X**
X	**21** **And When He Speaks, He Reminds Me to Eat** • Carmina Burana is a cantata by Carl Orff, based upon a series of Medieval poems (11th-13th century). Contrary to popular misconception, it is a secular composition	**22** **On Chaos Theory** • Dr. Stephen H. Kellert described Chaos Theory as "the qualitative study of unstable aperiodic behavior in deterministic nonlinear systems". • Someone I love a lot is worried about free will	**23** **Cartoon Logic** • This poem references 1 Corinthians 13:14 • *Parallax* is defined as, the effect whereby the position or direction of an object appears to differ when viewed from different positions, or mechanisms
27 **On Being Graceful** • It has been reported the etymology of the word "corral" comes from the Spanish word *corro* (noun), or ring	**28** **And So** • This poem is part nightmare, part panic attack on the Moroccan coast	**29** **Laughing**	**X**
34 **Angel Said, "Black Girl, Birth World"** • I asked for a sign and I got one	**X**	**X**	**38** **The Net Rising Soundless as Night, the Birds' Cry Soundless** • I had to pray four months to receive this poem

Violence

On Comedy `41` • For many reasons, this is something I can't forget • The events that inspired this poem transpired between 2010 and 2014, eventually leading me to a stint in the Scottish stand-up comedy scene		**On Appetite** `42` • The etymology of companion can be broken into two parts: The *com-* in companion means "with." The second part comes from *panis*, the Latin word for bread or food. *Companion*, at its most literal, meant someone with whom you shared a meal • In bread-baking terms, "proofing" is the time period in fermentation when you allow bread dough to rise. It is also known as "proving"
I Think it's Wild that You Would Ever Expect Me to be Hungry Again `47`	`X`	**Boyish,** `49` • Someone I love a lot once wanted to be a sparrow
After Jackson Kicks the Life Out of the Living-room Table `54` • Julia Kristeva is a Bulgarian-French philosopher and theorist. She is known for her work in psychoanalysis, semiotics, and philosophical feminism—particularly surrounding theories of the maternal. • Jackson, you're the worst	**Sour Cherry** `55`	**GREAT BLACK HOPE** `56` • This poem spans, temporally, from the founding of Princeton University (1746) to Sojurner Truth's "Ain't I a Woman" speech (1851), to 2017 • The proto-Germanic etymology of "blessing" is to hallow, or mark with blood
On the Occasion I Were to Dream I Had Grown My Father's Teeth `61`	**Five Minutes After Fruition** `62` • *Regression to the mean*, in statistics, states that the greater deviation of a random variate from its average, the greater the probability the next measured variate will deviate less far—or, that an extreme event is likely to be followed by a less extreme event	`X`

43 A New Moon	**44** All Our Armies	**45** This Doesn't Look Life a Housecall • Roland Barthes' *A Lover's Discourse* (1977) is what we read before bed	**46** Year of the Rabbit Hole
50 Monday, at Finishing School	**51** Neighbors	**52** Two Birds, All Moon • The four rivers listed in this poem, the Limmat, Thames, Liffey, and Tay are in Switzerland, England, Ireland and Scotland, respectively • *La Vita Nouva* is a text by Dante Alleghieri, published in 1294	**53** Schema
X	**58** St. John's Wort	**59** Cartoon Violence • This poem begins in medias res	**60** January 10th: 2014 • The title of this poem is based on The World is a Beautiful Place and I am No Longer Afraid to Die song of the same name. The song is a tribute to "Diana, Hunter of the Bus Drivers", a vigilante from Juraez, Mexico, who allegedly murdered two bus drivers in retaliation of the rape of two female factory workers, en route to work
64 Crawling Toward Collina d'Oro	**65** It's a Love Poem • This is not a happy love poem		

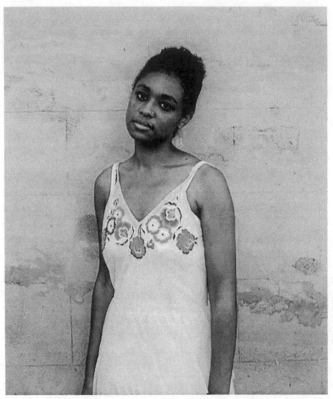

Photo Credit: Mollye Miller Photography

Alexus Erin is an American poet, performer, and Ph.D. candidate living in the UK. Her poetry has previously appeared in *Potluck Magazine, The Melanin Collective, The Nervous Breakdown, The Audacity, American Society of Young Poets, God Is in the TV, LEVELER, Red Flag Poetry, Silk + Smoke,* and a host of others. She is the author of two chapbooks: *Two Birds, All Moon* (Gap Riot Press, 2019) and *St. John's Wort* (Animal Heart Press, 2019). She was the 2018 Poetry Fellow of the Leopardi Writers Conference and a performer at Edinburgh Fringe Festival.

A note on the cover artist: Kimberly Seto Gordon is a special educator, future speech language pathologist, and maker of many things. Kimberly heard of, met and befriended Alexus, the mysterious accomplished author, during their time at college. For Kimberly to contribute her art as a part of Alexus's work truly means so much to her and their friendship. She currently lives in Los Angeles, California, with her fiancé and their kitten, Bubba.

The headers of *Cartoon Logic, Cartoon Violence* are set in
Bambi Bold by Gerard Bernor, a serif font similar
to the one used in the Disney movie *Bambi*.

The body text is set in Book Antiqua, a Roman typeface
based on pen-drawn letters of the Italian Renaissance.

Any body, suspended

Any in motion

intervenes, passing through.

Solid matter = time required

Capture, unbroken, gravity.

Negated by fear, certain bodies

pass through solid walls

Others cannot—

violent rearrangement,

impermanent

We need the relief

instead